CHEYENNE

Big Buddy Books
An Imprint of Abdo Publishing
www.abdopublishing.com

Sarah Tieck

www.abdopublishing.com

Published by Abdo Publishing, a division of ABDO, PO Box 398166, Minneapolis, Minnesota 55439.
Copyright © 2015 by Abdo Consulting Group, Inc. International copyrights reserved in all countries. No part
of this book may be reproduced in any form without written permission from the publisher. Big Buddy Books™
is a trademark and logo of Abdo Publishing.

Printed in the United States of America, North Mankato, Minnesota.
052014
092014

Cover Photo: © Rosanne Tackaberry/Alamy.
Interior Photos: © age fotostock/Alamy (p. 5); ASSOCIATED PRESS (p. 9); De Agostini/Getty Images (p. 27); Getty
      Images (pp. 19, 25); © Dan Leeth/Alamy (p. 25); © NativeStock.com/AngelWynn (pp. 15, 16, 17); © North Wind
      Picture Archives/Alamy (p. 23); © nsf/Alamy (p. 30); © Prisma Bildagentur AG/Alamy (p. 29); Shutterstock
      (pp. 11, 13, 21, 26).

Coordinating Series Editor: Rochelle Baltzer
Contributing Editors: Megan M. Gunderson, Marcia Zappa
Graphic Design: Adam Craven

Library of Congress Cataloging-in-Publication Data

Tieck, Sarah, 1976-
  Cheyenne / Sarah Tieck.
     pages cm. -- (Native Americans)
  ISBN 978-1-62403-353-7
  1. Cheyenne Indians--Juvenile literature. I. Title.
  E99.C53T54 2015
  978.004'97353--dc23
                          2014002719

CONTENTS

Amazing People

Hundreds of years ago, North America was mostly wild, open land. Native Americans lived on the land. They had their own languages and **customs**.

The Cheyenne (sheye-AN) are one Native American nation. They are known for their powerful hunters and Sun Dancers. Let's learn more about these Native Americans.

Some say the name *Cheyenne* comes from the Sioux and means "relatives of the Cree."

CHEYENNE TERRITORY

Before 1700, the Cheyenne lived in present-day Minnesota near Lake Superior. Later, the nation settled in what is now North Dakota, South Dakota, Montana, Wyoming, and Nebraska. On the plains, they became nomadic.

In the early 1800s, some Cheyenne moved to present-day Colorado. The nation split into northern and southern parts.

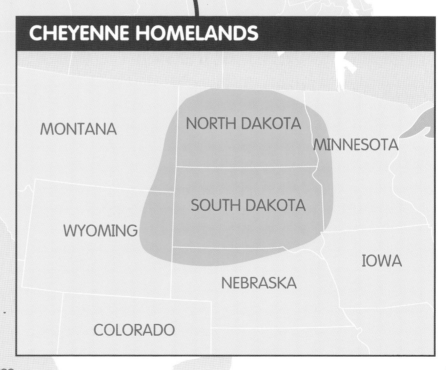

CANADA

UNITED STATES

MEXICO

N
W · E
S

CHEYENNE HOMELANDS

MONTANA

NORTH DAKOTA

MINNESOTA

SOUTH DAKOTA

WYOMING

IOWA

NEBRASKA

COLORADO

Home Life

   The Cheyenne way of life changed over the years. For a time, they lived in earth lodges. Once the tribe became nomadic, they lived in teepees.

   Teepees were made of buffalo skins that covered long wooden poles. The Cheyenne built a small fire in the center of each teepee. They used it to cook and keep warm. Smoke escaped through a hole at the top.

 Teepees were easy to move. They could be taken down or put up quickly.

WHAT THEY ATE

Early on, the Cheyenne were mostly hunters and farmers. They hunted deer and bear. They grew beans, corn, and squash. They also gathered wild rice and caught fish.

After the tribe moved to the plains, they rode horses to hunt buffalo. They sometimes ate wild turnips, berries, and even prickly pear cactus. They also traded goods with settlers for food.

Did You Know?

Today, there are about 20,000 wild buffalo on the plains. But, back when the Cheyenne hunted, there were millions!

There are many kinds of squash.
They can be stored for months to eat.

Did You Know?

Men mainly hunted buffalo. But, Cheyenne women sometimes helped drive the buffalo together.

On the plains, the American bison, or buffalo, was the most important food source. The tribe followed buffalo herds. They worked together to drive the buffalo into a group. Then, they used spears or bows and arrows to kill them.

Buffalo were not just hunted for food. The Cheyenne used other parts of the animal to make clothing, homes, tools, and containers.

Buffalo hunters were brave because these animals are huge! A full-grown male might be more than ten feet (3 m) long. It can weigh 2,000 pounds (900 kg)!

Daily Life

The Cheyenne were a huge nation of people spread across the plains. They lived in camps. People had different jobs. Men were warriors, hunters, or chiefs. Women ran the camps, cooked meals, and took care of the children. Both men and women made art.

Children learned by watching their parents. They played with toys that helped them prepare for adult life.

Did You Know?

Most Cheyenne warriors were men. But, some were women. This was unusual at that time in history.

 Boys practiced shooting bows and arrows. Girls played with deerskin dolls.

15

MADE BY HAND

The Cheyenne made clothes, such as deerskin dresses, war shirts, and leggings. They made moccasins to cover their feet. They also made tools and other objects. Their arts and crafts added beauty to everyday life.

Peace Pipes

The Cheyenne carved beautiful, long pipes. Some had parts made of stone, such as pipestone. The pipes were used in sacred ceremonies.

Beading

The Cheyenne decorated their clothes and bags with beads. Sometimes the beads, patterns, or colors had special meanings.

Quill Embroidery

The Cheyenne softened porcupine quills. Then they dyed them and wove them into leather for clothing. War shirts often took more than a year to complete!

SPIRIT LIFE

Religion was important to the Cheyenne way of life. The people believed there were two main spirits. These were the Wise One Above and a god who lived underground.

To honor spirits, the Cheyenne did special dances and held **ceremonies**. They followed certain laws and practices so the spirits would take care of their people. Every year, they did a Sun Dance after the long winter.

During the Sun Dance, the Cheyenne asked the spirits for guidance.

19

STORYTELLERS

Cheyenne men and women told stories. Some stories taught people history and lessons. Others were told just for fun! Storytelling was a way to pass on ideas and beliefs to younger tribe members.

The Cheyenne had short and long stories. There were war stories and **sacred** stories. The sacred stories were told at night. Often, many related stories were told in a row.

Did You Know?

The Cheyenne spoke an Algonquian language.

The Cheyenne often told stories over a feast or at a gathering.

Fighting for Land

The Cheyenne were forced off their land many times over the years. They eventually became **nomadic** and settled into life on the plains. Land was very important to the plains tribes. So, they often fought over it.

In the mid-1800s, gold was discovered near Cheyenne land. Then, the US government and American settlers took the land and its **resources**.

Did You Know?

Cheyenne chief Dull Knife led his people in a fight for their land. He was forced to move many times to reservations. He died in 1883.

 Black Kettle was a famous Cheyenne chief. He worked to make peace between his people and the US government. He died in 1868 when Lieutenant Colonel George Custer attacked his camp.

The Cheyenne, the US government, and American settlers had many battles over land. Settlers killed more buffalo than they needed. The government took other resources. It forced the Cheyenne to live on reservations. There, many people struggled because the land was different and the conditions were poor.

In 1876, the Cheyenne famously fought US soldiers in the Battle of the Little Bighorn. There were other smaller fights as they were forced to move to reservations.

Did You Know?

Today, the Northern Cheyenne have a reservation in southern Montana. The Southern Cheyenne have a reservation in Oklahoma.

 At the Battle of the Little Bighorn, Cheyenne and Sioux joined to fight US Lieutenant Colonel George Custer (*above*). Custer and his men died. So, this battle is also called "Custer's Last Stand."

 In 1864, US soldiers attacked the Cheyenne and Arapaho at Sand Creek, Colorado. Today, people remember the 150 to 200 Native Americans who died in this attack.

Back in Time

About 1700

The Cheyenne moved to North Dakota. Over time, they began hunting buffalo and became **nomadic**.

Before 1700

The Cheyenne lived in the area around Lake Superior in what is now Minnesota. They hunted and farmed there.

Early 1800s

The Cheyenne separated into northern and southern groups.

1876

The Cheyenne and the Sioux fought against US Army troops led by Lieutenant Colonel George Custer. It became known as the Battle of the Little Bighorn, or "Custer's Last Stand."

1884

The US government gave the Northern Cheyenne a **reservation** in Montana.

2010

The US government counted about 11,000 Cheyenne living in the country.

A Strong Nation

The Cheyenne people have a long, rich history. They are remembered for their buffalo hunting skills and their powerful fighters. They are also known for strong leaders, such as Black Kettle and Dull Knife.

Cheyenne roots run deep. Today, the people keep alive those special things that make them Cheyenne. Even though times have changed, many people carry the **traditions**, stories, and memories of the past into the present.

Cheyenne people of all ages gather for events, such as the Red Earth Festival in Oklahoma.

29

"All we ask is to be allowed to live, and live in peace. I seek no war with anyone. An old man, my fighting days are done."

— Dull Knife

GLOSSARY

ceremony a formal event on a special occasion.

custom a practice that has been around a long time and is common to a group or a place.

nomadic of or relating to people that travel from place to place.

reservation (reh-zuhr-VAY-shuhn) a piece of land set aside by the government for Native Americans to live on.

resource a supply of something useful or valued.

sacred (SAY-kruhd) connected with worship of a god.

tradition (truh-DIH-shuhn) a belief, a custom, or a story handed down from older people to younger people.

WEBSITES

To learn more about Native Americans, visit **booklinks.abdopublishing.com**. These links are routinely monitored and updated to provide the most current information available.

INDEX